· MY · FIRST · LOOK · AT ·

Shapes

[DK]

DORLING KINDERSLEY

London • New York • Stuttgart

Circles

yo-yo

softball

flower

clock

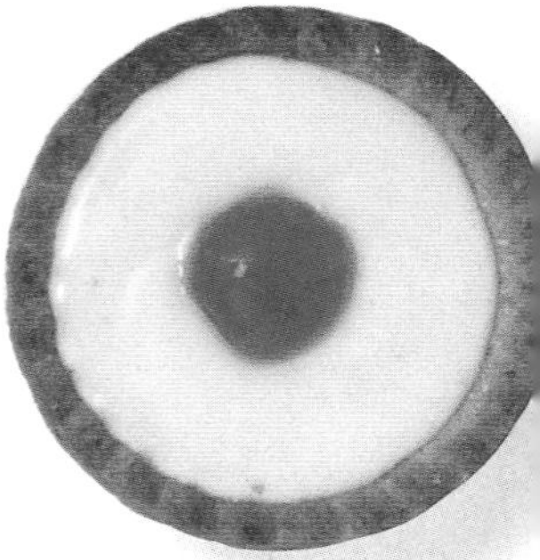

cake

beads

biscuits

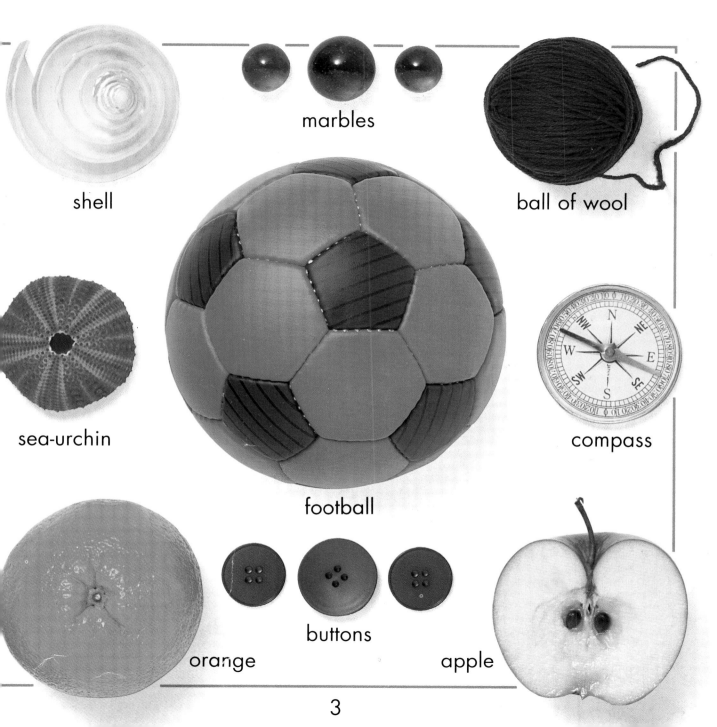

shell

marbles

ball of wool

sea-urchin

football

compass

orange

buttons

apple

3

Triangles

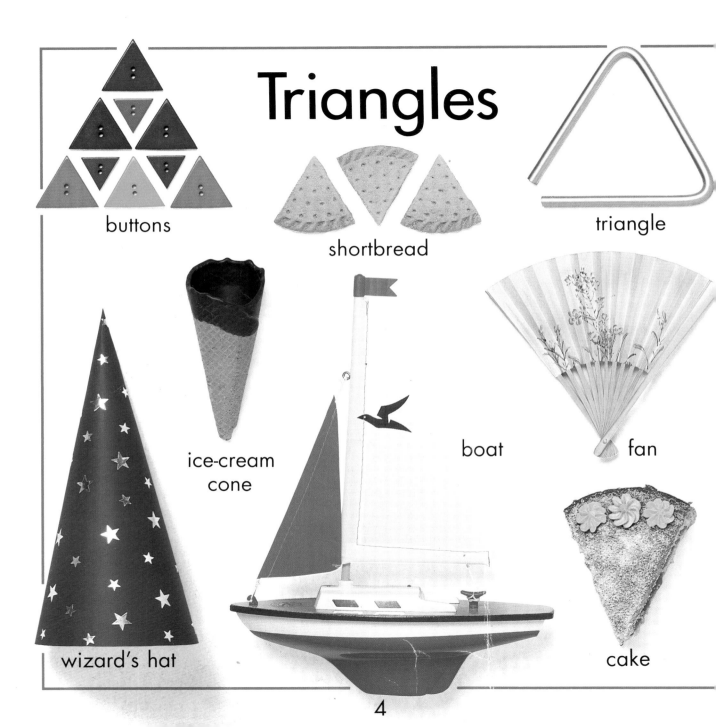

buttons

shortbread

triangle

ice-cream cone

boat

fan

wizard's hat

cake

4

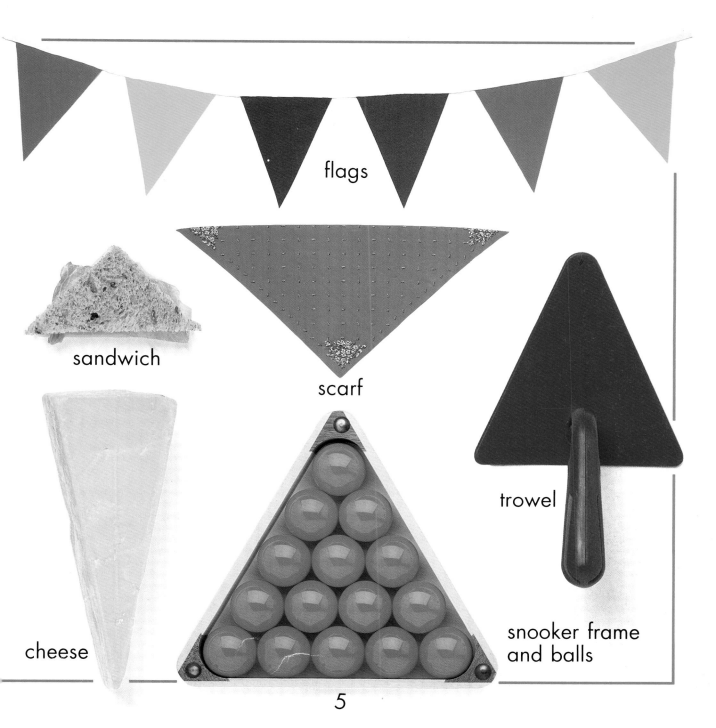

flags

sandwich

scarf

cheese

snooker frame
and balls

trowel

5

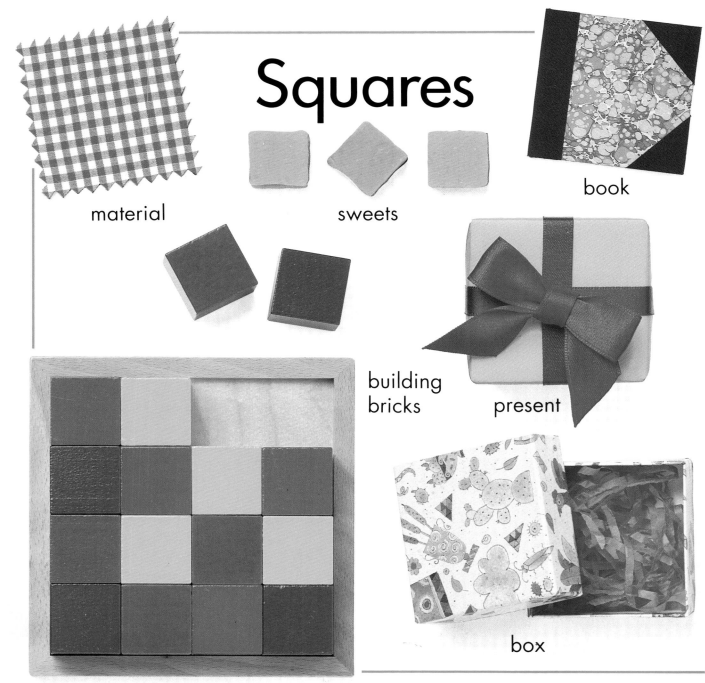

Squares

material

sweets

book

building bricks

present

box

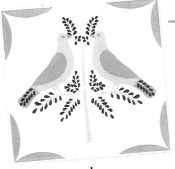

tile

dice

handkerchief

pincushion

clock

jack-in-the-box

fabric picture bricks

Rectangles

bag

hair-slide

chocolate bar

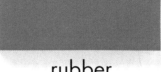

rubber

shoe box

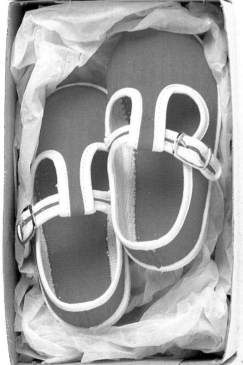

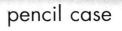

pencil case

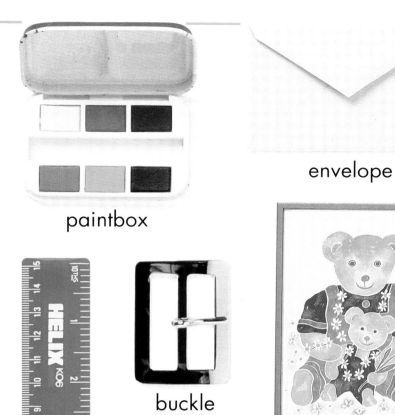

paintbox

envelope

biscuit

buckle

picture

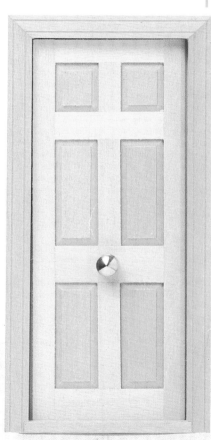

ruler

brick

door

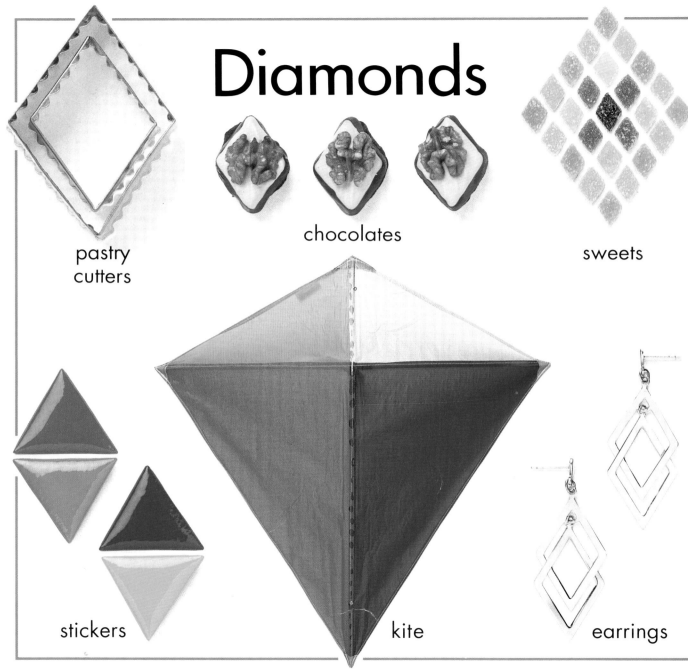

Diamonds

pastry
cutters

chocolates

sweets

stickers

kite

earrings

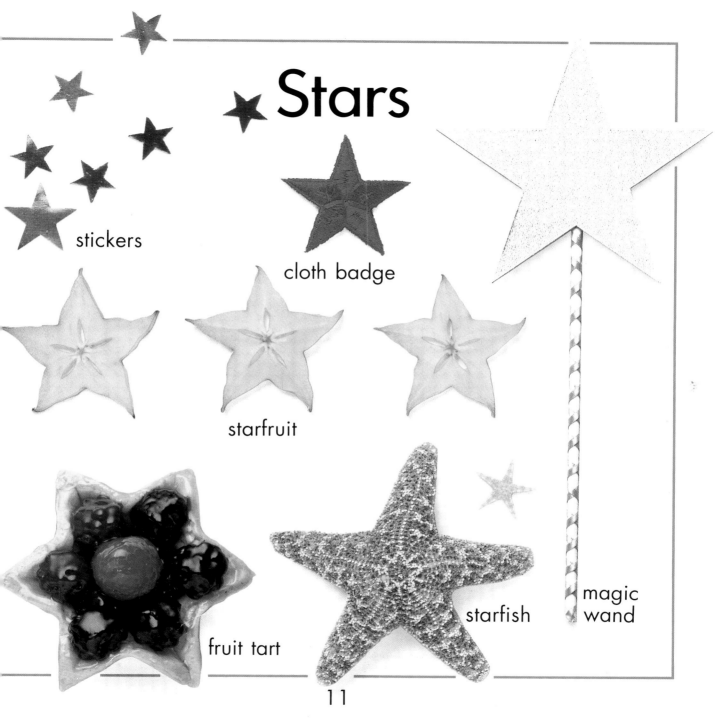

Stars

stickers

cloth badge

starfruit

fruit tart

starfish

magic wand

11

Rings

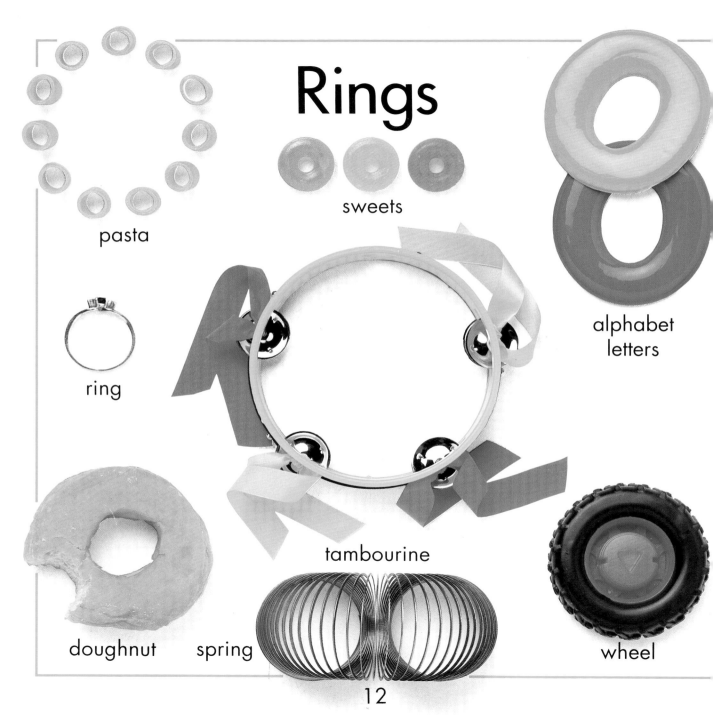

pasta

sweets

alphabet letters

ring

doughnut

tambourine

spring

wheel

12

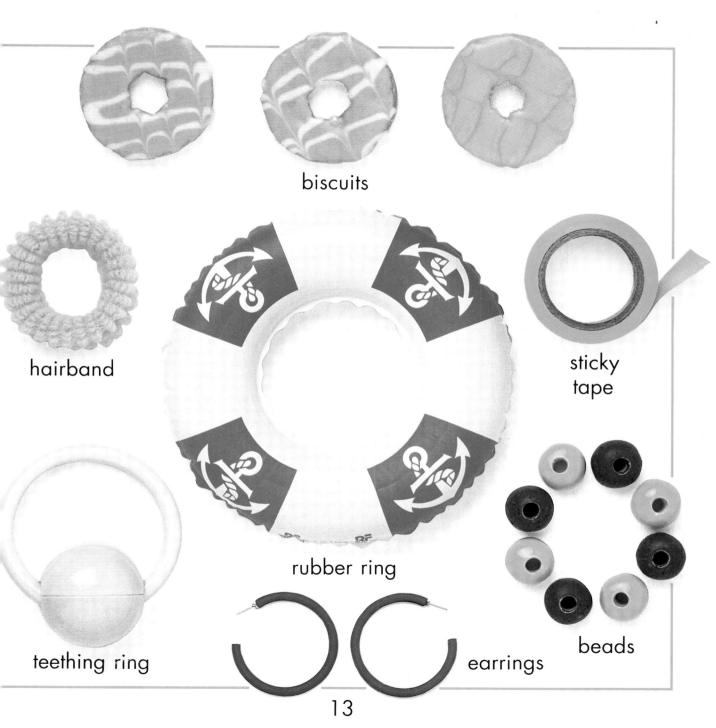

biscuits

hairband

sticky tape

rubber ring

teething ring

earrings

beads

13

Ovals

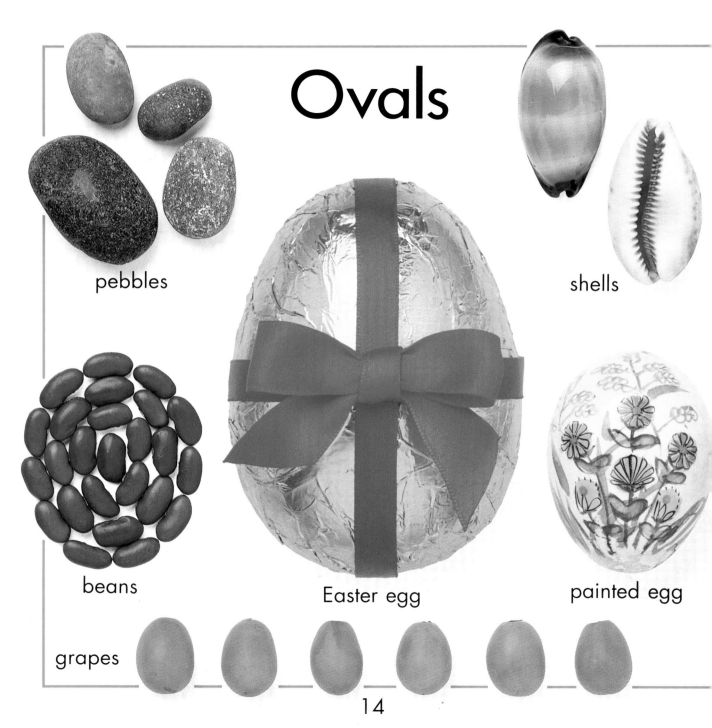

pebbles

shells

beans

Easter egg

painted egg

grapes

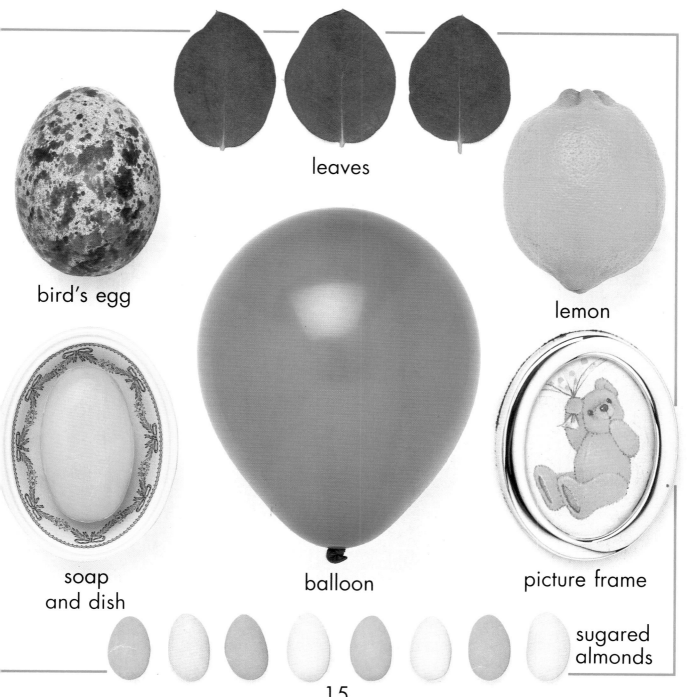

bird's egg

leaves

lemon

soap
and dish

balloon

picture frame

sugared
almonds

15

Hearts

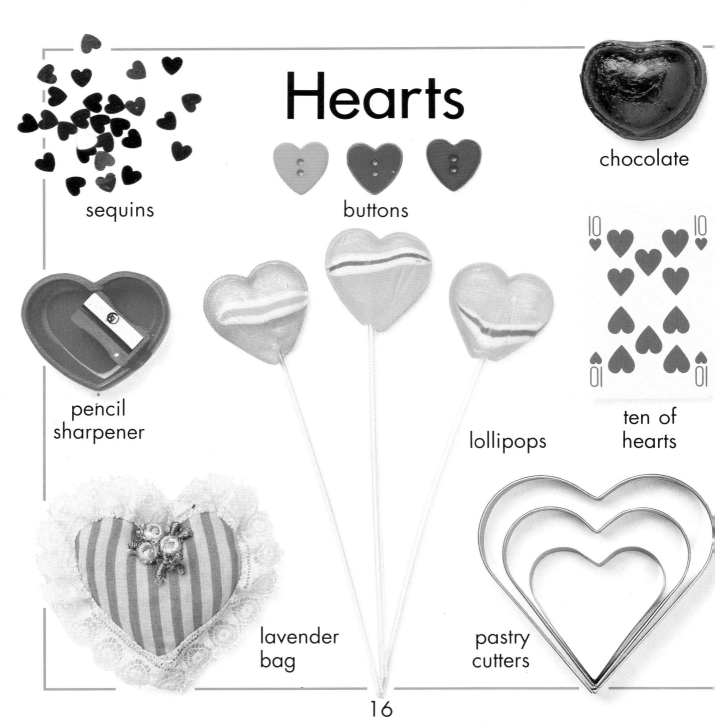

sequins

buttons

chocolate

pencil
sharpener

lollipops

ten of
hearts

lavender
bag

pastry
cutters

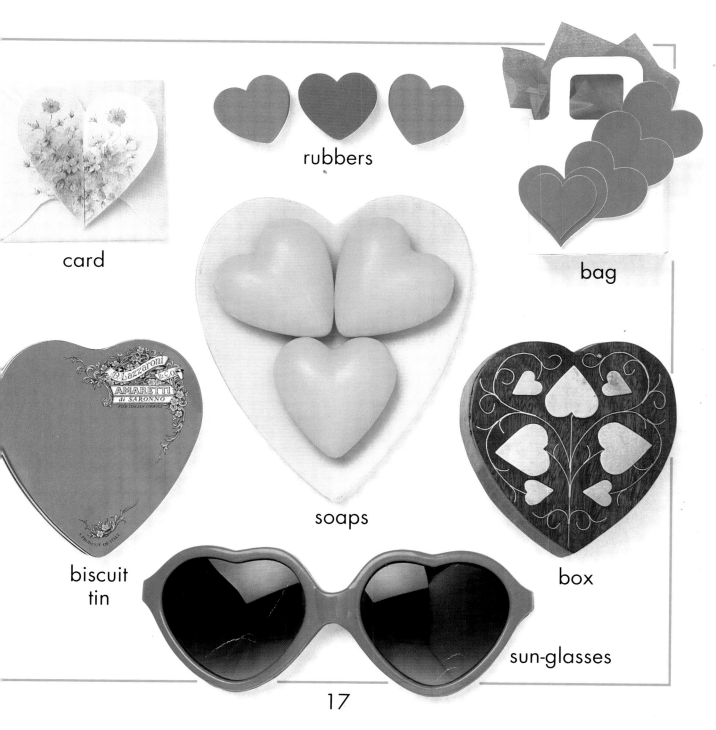

card

rubbers

bag

soaps

biscuit tin

box

sun-glasses

17

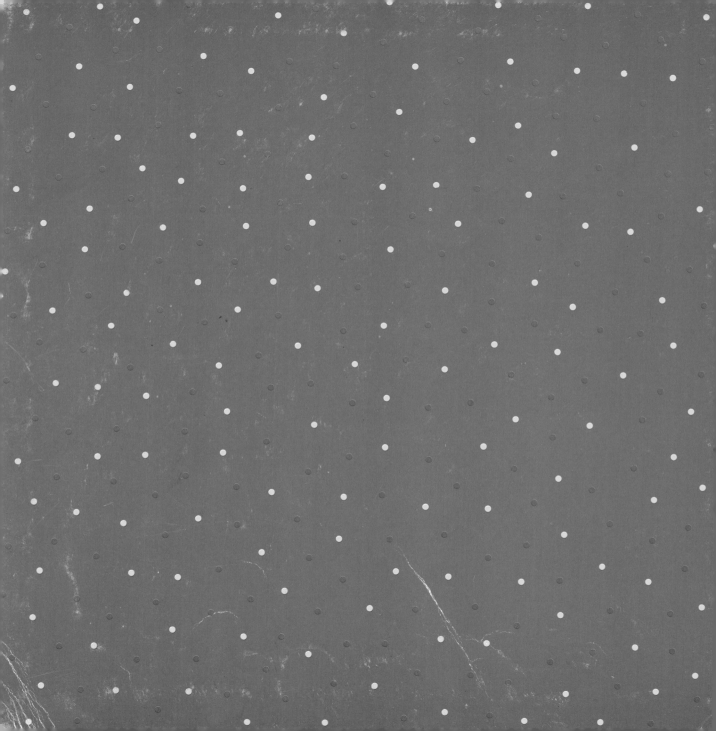